HOLD 'EM

ADVANCED

HOLD 'EM

ADVANCED

BY ANDY NELSON

PokerBook Press
Boulder, Colorado

HOLD 'EM: ADVANCED
By Andy Nelson

ISBN 0-945983-04-2

Manufactured in the United States of America

First Printing - April, 1996

First Edition

10 9 8 7 6 5 4 3 2 1

TABLE OF CONTENTS

INTRODUCTION

Does it seem strange to you that someone would write an advanced book on low-limit Texas Hold 'Em? Isn't it an oxymoron to place "advanced" and "low-limit" together? If you are an advanced player, why would you play low-limit? Doesn't an advanced book on any kind of poker automatically assume the reader will be playing higher stakes poker?

In one form or another, these questions have been asked of me many times. My response is that I clearly see a strong market for an advanced book on low-limit Texas Hold 'Em. I personally know many players who want to know all they possibly can about low-limit Texas Hold 'Em before they try to move up to the higher stakes games. In their minds, they are willing to pay the price of a longer apprenticeship to become well grounded in the fundamentals of Texas Hold 'Em. They are willing to climb the mountain slowly so they will know deep in their hearts and minds they have a solid foundation. They will know that they know. Knowing that they know will give them confidence that will make them winners at all levels of play.

BEATING THE LOW-LIMIT GAME

You will notice that throughout the book, I am making the assumption that you, the reader, are the best player at whatever low-limit table you chose. Building on that concept, it has been my experience that the toughest game to beat is low-limit poker. Low-limit poker places a limitation on the good player. In low-limit you give up one of the basic weapons in your arsenal, the power of money. It is seldom that you can use money to intimidate in a low-limit game. The good poker player has a number of effective weapons that he brings to the table: knowledge of the odds, knowledge of people, the power of observation, emotional stability, confidence and betting courage. These are just some of the weapons that the quality player uses to win consistently.

My belief is that if you buy this book, you are a serious Texas Hold 'Em player and you want to be the best you can be. My point in this section is that everyone who plays low-limit poker gives up the use of money as an intimidation factor. Intimidation is a potent factor in poker. If you give up the power of intimidation with money, it also means the other players cannot intimidate you with their money. Therefore the playing ground is more or less even. However, consider this: If you are the best player, any limitation, such as taking away the power of money, will limit you more than it will limit a lesser player.

WHAT IS AN ADVANCED PLAYER?

I can hear you say, "What is an advancecd player? That is a good question, Andy. In your opinion, what constitutes an advanced versus a good intermediate player? Give us a geography lesson here, Andy. What are the boundaries of beginner, the intermediate and the advanced player?"

Ah, yes. An advanced player. What is it? Who is it? Are you one? Is that guy in the middle of the table an advanced player? An intermediate player? What are the factors that make up a quality player? What does one need in order to call himself/herself an advanced player? Let me give you my considered opinion and you balance it with what you think.

THE BEGINNING PLAYER

This category is fairly easy. It begins with a person learning the rank of hands, four-of-a-kind beats a full house, a flush beats a straight and a straight beats three of a kind, etc. The good beginning player will learn the basic mathematics, have a pretty good starting hand selection technique worked out, be aware of the power of position, have a fair idea of what hands can be played from what position, and the start of a betting strategy. The beginning player will have some actual experience at the table. It is not nearly enough to read books, run poker software and watch videos. The school room is the green felt table where the rudimentary lessons are hammered into the brain. Experience plus study will move the observant player along.

THE INTERMEDIATE PLAYER

Where is the line between beginning play and intermediate play? One important criteria is for the intermediate player to know "Why" he or she plays a certain hand. That *why* is basic to his win rate: "Why" this hand and not that hand in this set of circumstances. Quite often the very same hand can be played in one situation and not in another. "Why?" That why question is essential for the person who would call himself an intermediate player.

The player who would be an intermediate player will start to recognize trap hands and trap situations. The refinement of avoiding traps comes at the advanced level, but it will have its beginning at the intermediate level.

The intermediate player will have well-defined betting strategies. Again, he or she will have an answer to the "Why?" of making a certain bet or raise. Unlike the beginner, who just wings it because it feels good, the intermediate player will have a well-defined reason.

Skill at reading other players will start to come into focus for the intermediate player. He will be paying more and more attention to how others play, what patterns they have, what tells can be picked up. This skill of reading players is an important factor in the development of the poker player.

Another essential lesson to be learned is patience. The intermediate player has developed patience. He knows that he cannot win unless he waits for the winning hand to come his way. He has learned the lesson that he cannot push a moderate hand through to win the pot. Low-limit poker does not work that way. He must wait for the best hand and maximize his win through skillful betting. Here the key word is *patience*.

The last item in this list of conceptss I want to stress does not complete the differences, but it does give the essential factors. The last item the intermediate player develops is emotional control. This clearly separates the intermediate from the beginner. Poker is an emotional game. That is a fact. Just watch the faces and action of the players at any poker game. You will see an incredible variety of emotions. Unless one has a good handle on what one is feeling, he or she could become his or her own worst enemy. The intermediate player has begun the process of emotional control.

THE ADVANCED PLAYER

The advanced player is the person who is well on his way to mastering his craft. First, above all things, is his emotional control. Seldom does he or she get upset or go on tilt. He truly accepts the idiosyncrasies of low-limit poker. When another player makes an incredibly bad move (for example, he calls a couple of raises with a 2-7 offsuit and wins the pot against our hero who has pocket aces and flops the top set), the advanced player just eases back in his chair and waits for the next opportunity to take down a pot. He does not allow such juvenile play to distress him. He knows that this is part of low-limit poker. He agrees to compete in the low-limit arena and take his chances.

Another area the advanced player is competent in is reading other players. He has worked on this part of his game and understands some of the complexities of the human animal. He knows that when a player sits down at the poker table, he quite often allows his ego to guide his play rather than his intellect. The advanced player is quite capable of taking advantage of that man. The advanced player also understands and profits from the complexities of male and female interaction. He is also competent to turn a profit from that interaction. Some male players are reluctant to bet into, raise or check raise a pretty woman. When you see that happening, it allows you to play a marginal hand a bit longer. Careful observations might give you a second chance to win the pot.

Based upon his observations of people, combined with the intricate and endless possibilities of how the flop affects a person's hand, the advanced player has learned to read many, many things that the beginner and intermediate player is not able to see. The flop is terribly important. No, let me change that: *The flop is incredibly important.* The flop has a powerful impact upon the play of each and every hand. Since there are often six or seven players who see the flop in each hand, the complexities are enormous. This is the arena that becomes the learning ground for the astute player. He combines the physical properties (the card denominations and suits) of the flop with the emotional potentialities of the players to discover if he can turn a profit from that hand. He carefully watches the betting patterns and reactions of opponents. His brain seeks out reasons for every action and reaction. He builds his storehouse of information on each player. This is where skill pays off at the cashiers cage. This is what advanced play is about. Plain and simple, advanced play is a careful study of card combinations and human combinations.

CHAPTER ONE

EMOTIONAL CONTROL

In my opinion, nothing demonstrates the difference between intermediate play and advance poker play more clearly than emotional control. This is where the line is clearly drawn. If you allow the bad play of other players to control or to change your play, you are allowing the game to control you. The advanced player knows his game, knows his own play and charts his own course. No one changes that course. No one. The winds of change may try to blow him off course, to buffet him about. The flow of the cards can change from great to terrible to horrible. The reprobate down at the other end may do his very best to upset him. These things happen with regularity, but the advanced player is aware of them happening and refuses to allow them to affect him. He knows who he is and will not allow these negative forces to penetrate his psyche. He is who he is. His shield turns away the arrows that would do him harm. His armor is his self-confidence and trust in himself.

Okay, that is easy to write but I am also preaching to myself as I write. There have been a few occasions where I have slipped and let my emotions get away from me. Recently I raised in late position with this hand:

The flop came:

That is a great flop for my hand. It was checked to me and I bet. After all I had the top pair with the second best kicker. This is certainly not a lock but I believe I had the best hand at the moment. When I have the best hand, I want to make the others pay money to run me down. Four people called. Nothing unusual there. The next card was:

There was still nothing to be real concerned about. This time I got two callers. The next card was:

A guy across the table bet. I could feel my anger start to fester. Could he have played an Ace this long? The thought crossed my mind that he had played an Ace-eight and caught two pairs. That is fairly common. I had to see what he had. He had the Ace of diamonds and the four of clubs! He had absolutely nothing on the flop, nothing on the turn except a possible pair. And even his kicker was horrible. I lost it at this point. I asked him sarcastically what he had on the flop. Then I asked him what he had on the turn. He just shrugged and continued to stack my chips. I went to the bathroom and washed my face. See what I mean about low-limit poker?

BE THE PATRICIAN

In observing of my actions and those of others, I find the biggest source of irritation is the bad play of others that defeats us. We seem to approve of bad play as long as the bad player loses the pot. The anger comes when they play badly and take down the pot.

One of the identifying factors that allows one to point out an advanced player is the attitude, the demeanor of the player. His or her face is relaxed, completely in charge of his or her fate. There is no anxiety evident. Is that how you appear at the table? If not, you need to work on it.

I am reminded of the mature athlete, like the old pro basketball player who takes the floor, shoots a few warmup shots, stretches a bit and is ready to go. The games ebb and flow. Sometimes he scores a lot of points, sometimes not. His attitude is whatever will be will be. If he doesn't score big this game, it is okay as long as the team wins. The point is, while doing everything in his power to win, he looks relaxed and assured. When the game is on the line, often called crunch time, he will clearly demonstrate his skill.

Another example of patrician behavior is that of an experienced and successful relief pitcher in the biggs. He can throw smoke and he knows he will get the batter out. Just the way he walks to the mound tells everyone in the ball park that he is "the man." There is not doubt. The intimidation factor is incredible. The intimidation factor is what you want working for you.

How does one become the patrician? The answer is quite simple: plain old hard work. The old-fashioned way, long and hard labor. Intimidating knowledge of the game does not come quickly or without effort. If you put in the time and energy, it will come. That is the price that one must pay to become the patrician. There are many, many plebes and wannabees. The plebes and wannabees are the people who will feed and support the patrician. The line of demarkation between the plebe and the patrician is the desire and the ability to put in the time and effort needed to understand the game.

THE PATRICIAN'S EMOTIONAL CONTROL

When you truly understand the game of Hold 'Em, your emotions will smooth out. The bad-beat horror stories that others tell will be a thing of the past for you. It isn't that the bad-beats won't happen to you. They will indeed happen. That is the nature of low-limit poker. Bad-beats go with the territory. The difference is that those dreaded beats won't affect you like they did. After all, you are the patrician, the master of the game. You know they will happen and accept beats as a part of the game. A plebe will whine and gripe. The patrician will softly smile and wait for the next hand. He knows his turn will come and so he waits, hoping the guy who made the long shot will stay long enough for the patrician to get his money back and more. He knows that Joe Cool will take home the money more often than Nervous Ned or Anxious Andy.

QUALITY PLAY

There are some experienced players who mistakenly believe they can be aggressive enough to force a hand. Unfortunately, in low-limit poker this is not often true. Sure, once in a while it will work to bet a hand like crazy and everyone will fold. However, we have all seen it where the novice player will bet and when he gets raised, will look puzzled, peek back at his cards, think for a moment and then dump in the money. He doesn't know that he is supposed to get out. He has a draw or a pair and by damn, he is just playing the hand out. The cost does not phase him. The fact that the experienced player is trying to intimidate him with the force of his money and with his personality doesn't compute for the novice. Strong betting a poor or marginal hand in low-limit poker is just not effective in the long term. Unsophisticated players will simply call the hand down. Aggressive play does not mean you play poor cards and try to force them to become winners. The advanced player knows this and does not attempt to use the tool of money power against the novice. He has the emotional control to wait his turn, play only quality cards, and try to max out the hand when he has the winner.

BACKBONE OF STEEL

The advanced player knows that his knowledge of the game will win for him eventually. He knows that it is adversity that is the stone that hones his skills to razor-sharp edge. Anyone can look like a world class player when he is catching cards. When the dealer pushes pot after pot to a player who makes marginal plays and wins, the advanced player knows the string will be short lived. When the lucky player hits that one in 47 shot to take the money, our hero will shrug it off and say, "Good hand, sir." His backbone is rigid, his emotions solid and his head is on straight. There is no wishbone where is backbone ought to be. Time is on the good player's side. The dragon will be slain even when it looks like all the chips are headed for the other end of the table. Emotional control is the identifying factor of the advanced player.

A STEADY HAND WINS THE MONEY

Who hasn't seen the grouch who slams his fist down on the table? Or the one who will throw his cards at the dealer? Or curse the dealer? Or any number of other actions that indicate that he or she is emotionally upset? When you see that happening, you know for sure that player is not an advanced player. Throwing your cards or chips is a sure sign of emotional immaturity.

I am well aware that poker is an emotional game. I have done quite a number of crazy things in my poker career. I know well the violent responses one can have while participating in a game. More than once I have wanted to fight a player who beat me and then said something derogatory to me. I went through a period when I would pound the table with my fist after I lost a hand. Slowly, as I learned what this game is about, my behavior changed. Once in a while something will upset me but almost all the time my composure is pretty good.

One thing I am thankful for is that seldom can another player put me on tilt by saying disparaging things. Once a guy challenged me by giving me a couple of insults. After the second one, I just quietly said, "If you have a problem with me or my play, see the chaplain." He knew he had done his best to push me and I was telling him in language he could understand that pushing would do no good, so just shut up. He did.

Once while playing in a satellite tournament in Las Vegas, one of the players at my table picked up his chair and was going to hit the dealer with it. I grabbed the chair and security grabbed the guy. That is the sort of emotion that poker will elicit. Deep, deep stuff that borders on jungle behavior. Somehow our ego or our survival seems to be at stake and we will react very strongly. Don't be afraid of these emotions when you feel them. Work on learning to control them. Learn how to call them by name and how to channel them into productive areas like study of the cards or people. Focus on developing your intimate awareness of

17

how other people feel and how to utilize that information in your game plan.

Emotional control is an incredibly vital tool to have if you want to move up to the advanced class. Without emotional control you will not make a successful low-limit poker player. Those are the facts of the case. You either have emotional control or you will not win long term. It takes a long time to perfect emotional control but you have no other choice if you want to win.

CHAPTER TWO

PLAYING THE CARDS

In the play of the cards, the story of advanced play is far more than solid hand selection. Solid hand selection is one of the qualities that mark a good intermediate player. The advanced player goes several steps beyond. Even at the low-limit level the advanced player will mix up his play in effective ways. In his hand selection he won't do foolish things like consistently raise with draw hands like medium suited connectors or the low pocket pairs. Once in a while he will throw in a raise with those kinds of hands, and if he catches the right flop will show the players a move that will surprise and confuse them. The advanced players have mastered the art of good hand selection. For the most part, the advanced player's skill generally comes into play after the flop.

WHAT DOES THE FLOP TELL YOU?

Advanced play has much more to do with reading the flop than basic hand selection. This is where the skill of good poker begins to pay off. Make no mistake, effectively reading the flop in low-limit poker is a chancy business! These players will do the darndest things. I have seen players play a hand like Q♣–3♥ in early position and call two raises when the action gets back to them. If the flop should come with a couple of threes, they have a powerful hand.

I was playing in a tournament and raised with Big Slick. The flop came:

I was counting the chips out there in the center when a guy raised me. What the hell could he have that could beat me? Well, he had called my raise cold with a King-four! Offsuit! In a tournament! See what I mean? Low-limit poker is a chancy business. I could read the flop well enough, I just could not believe anyone would play a four after a raise in the middle stages of a tournament. I should have been a tad more careful. Needless to say, that player busted out and I finished second.

The advanced player sees the complexities and the possibilities that are presented on the flop. He is aware of how the flop helps or hurts his own hand and the hand(s) of his opponent(s). It is those possibilities that direct him in his betting strategies.

THE FLOP CARDS ARE KEY

Sixty percent of the information that you will get from the community cards come on the flop. Those three cards have an incredible impact on how or if you will play this hand. When you compute in the total amount of information that each player has after the flop, you will find that each player has 71.5% of the total information on your own hand. Over 70% of the total is now available! Five of the total of seven cards are now visible to you. How you process that information will be a big factor in your success. Here are a few basic ideas on what to do with some of the more common situations. Because the number of possibilities are just too extensive, I am only able to use a few illustrations. I believe this will give you a road map to finding the more intricate situations that you can turn into profit. The first two examples are fairly uncomplicated.

FLOPPING THE TOP PAIR

Flopping the top pair is a common situation. This is a major source of profit for any Hold 'Em player. Usually you will be playing only the high cards in the deck and so the top pair will likely be a picture card or an Ace. The question is how best to play this to win the most money. Say you started with Big Slick:

The flop comes:

That is a great flop for that hand. You have top pair with the best kicker. If you should get an overcard, it will give you two pairs. Of course you will bet. If someone bets in front of you, you will naturally raise. Straightforward stuff. The person you want to get out is the one who came in with a hand like:

This player often will hang around hoping to catch a seven to make three-of-a-kind. A seven would be deadly for you but if an ace should come, you would have an ideal hand. Each of you would have two pairs, but yours is the top two pairs.

In low-limit Hold 'Em, there is no way on earth to get rid of the people with spade draws. So don't worry about them. You could pull the pin on a live grenade and throw it on the table and the spade draws would call. If a spade comes, you could very well take a beating. If two spades come, you might have a chance. Given the amount of money in the pot, the Ace of spades would not be a terrible scenario:

The flop looks like this:

The next card is:

Now you have top two pairs with the second nut flush draw. (It is extremely unlikely a player would be in there with the three-four, three-five or four-five of spades, but anything is possible in low-limit poker.) How many cards will help this hand? Two Aces and two Kings are live to give you the full house and nine spades will make a good flush. A total of thirteen outs, less the two spades that could be in someone else's hand, of course.

It isn't likely but you might get crushed between two made flushes that max out the betting, especially when you have the King of spades, but a whipsaw could be an expensive situation to be in. The pot odds will probably be in your favor, but it would be costly if you do not improve to the full house or the nut spades.

So where are you with flopping top pair like that? Not bad. You will lose some to flushes and sometimes to the player who will call and improve with an underpair. You have just as much chance to improve as the person drawing to the underpair, so don't fret the times you lose to them. There shouldn't be any straight draws out there after the flop, but in low-limit Hold 'Em you often find the guy who will draw for a draw. Say he has a hand like:

He calls and he catches a ten on the turn.

Now he wants a nine or an Ace on the river. So be aware that this draw for a draw to a straight can and does happen. That is why you hope somebody is playing a King-Queen in front of you and bets so that you can raise and get out the ribbon clerks who will draw for a draw.

AGAIN, TOP PAIR

What about hitting the top pair when you have played a hand in an unraised pot like:

and the flop is

Top pair with a jack kicker is a problem from several standpoints. This is not the time to rejoice, you have not won the pot. Any overcard is dangerous. But it is still better than catching a flop like:

Neither hand is a bed of pansies but the first flop is a tad better because you have an overcard in your hand.

The big danger is that either flop has made someone two pairs, either the ten-nine or the Jack-nine. There will be the usual draws of Queen-Jack, seven-eight, Queen-ten and ten-eight.

My betting strategy for this situation, when I flop top pair, is to bet if it is checked to me and raise if it is bet in front of me. If it is bet and raised in front of me, I am done with it unless the raiser is a person who will bet or raise with a draw. If the raise comes from a good player, I will put him on an Ace-ten or two pairs. Top pair with a moderate kicker is just not worth defending. There are too many better hands and overcards that can defeat me as well as the danger of someone making a straight. I want better odds before I invest much of my money in this situation.

27

TOP PAIR AGAINST STRAIGHT AND FLUSH DRAWS

Suppose you play that big slick hand. However, the flop comes,

That flop is dangerous. There are a bunch of cards that can beat you if they should come. Obviously all the clubs are danger cards. Also any ten, nine, eight, five, four and three can do you in with a straight. Twenty-four cards can put a straight beat on you. Any six or seven could easily give someone a set. Poker is fun, you say? I'm not saying that if any of those cards come you are beaten. They are scare cards to make you cautious.

My general theory of betting is to bet as hard as I can when I have top pair with a decent kicker. If someone has flopped a set or two pairs, maybe he will let me know before I invest any more money. You see, if I get raised, I will generally release the hand if the person who raised me is good player. If he or she is an average player, I will often re-raise to find out where they are at. Lots of average players will raise with an Ace and any kind of kicker. I love those guys. Believe me, I will make them pay to play an Ace with a poor kicker.

The big danger with flopping the top pair is having someone flop two pairs or a set. The better players will make you pay dearly and sometimes you are trapped into calling them down. The first thought that pops into my head when I get raised is "two pairs." Then I ask myself what two pairs are the most likely and do I think that player would play those cards? It is fact that flopping the top pair will often cost you some chips but in the long run, that hand will make you a lot of money. Make the turkeys chase you with their second and third pairs.

Let's talk about the situation where someone raises you when you have top pair with a decent kicker. What is the best policy? Usually the best course of action is to get a good fix on the player who did the raising. Is he or she the type of player who will raise on a draw? If not, is he or she the type of player who will raise with top pair and a poor kicker, say something like K♣-4♣, when a King hits the board? That kind of a raise happens

29

in low-limit. If the raiser is a decent player I will go back to my standard reaction of saying "two pairs" to myself. Now two things must be present for me to call the raise. One: There must be at least five dollars for every dollar I have to invest in the call. Two: My kicker must be higher than the lower two cards on the board. Let me illustrate.

Suppose I have played this hand:

The flop comes:

Suppose I placed the opening bet and a solid player raised me immediately. I did not believe this player would raise with a straight draw because he would want the other players to call and make the pot bigger so that if his straight got there he would win more money. I therefore had to put him on a hand like Ace-jack or Ace-nine. Now I would fold my hand because if I should hit my kicker, the eight, I would still lose. Not a pretty picture. Even the back door flush draw would not make me call unless there was a huge pot out there.

Flopping top pair with a weak kicker is a common occurrence. Sometimes you will play a hand like K♦-6♦ from late position if there are several callers and there has been no raise. I think one should look at the flop in that situation. Another common scenario is to have a Q♣-4♦ in the blind that has not been raised. The flop might come:

What should one do if there are, say, five active players? My thinking is to bet. There are three inside straight draws (J-T, 9-T, 9-J) so I figure that if I have the only Queen, most of them will fold. If a good player calls me, I'll check after the turn card unless I hit my kicker. If he bets, I will fold. I have risked enough on that cheese hand.

FLOPPING THE MONSTER

Once in a great while, you get really lucky and flop a huge hand. This is usually a pretty happy situation. Now you have a different problem. That problem is usually how to max out the hand. On rare occasions you will have a bad problem, that of running into an even better hand. Say you have this hand:

and you catch a flop like:

You have flopped the top full house. An absolutely beautiful hand. It will be very unlikely that you run into four Queens. It is even more rare for someone to catch a card that will make them a royal flush. It will happen occasionally. So be just a tad careful if you get back-raised by a very good player or get two raises from an average player. These are indications that your monster has found another monster. These are expensive encounters.

MAX THE HAND

The more common problem is trying to get the absolute most out of these fortunate situations. It does not happen often, but it is wonderful! When you cripple the deck like the hand above, you will often lose the better players. They will suspect something big and just get away from it. The players you want in there are the players with a Queen or a straight or flush draw. They will usually call at least one bet. The people who might hold a Queen could even raise you. That would be lovely, especially if they should fill up. My advice is to bet only once on the betting round after the flop. You don't want to lose the draws and you want to encourage the players that have a Queen to put in a raise. If someone should bet into you on the first betting round, do not raise. Try to trap them if you can. A lot of this depends upon your position. Each hand has to be carefully planned. These are golden opportunities. Make the most of them.

PLAYING SECOND PAIR

My first reaction to playing second pair after the flop is to say, "Never!" However, there are some situations where it is profitable. Pot odds is the best reason to play. If you are in a pot where there are several players and each player has invested a couple of bets before the flop and you catch the second pair, sometimes it is wise to see at least one card. Much depends on your position relative to the raisers. You don't want to invest much in drawing at the cards that will improve your hand: the two cards that will give you three of a kind and the three cards that will make you two pairs. There are several considerations besides the pot odds and implied odds. The most important consideration at this point is if you should make two pairs, would that card make someone an even better hand? It is foolish to draw to a hand that will allow someone else to defeat you even when you make your hand. That is really dumb. Let me illustrate.

Suppose you play this hand:

 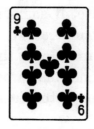

and the flop is:

You have flopped second pair but the problem is that there are two cards that will help your hand, the nine of hearts and the nine of spades. You certainly do not want the nine of hearts! And even any nine could make someone a straight. My advice: Dump the hand unless you are in late position and have to call only one betting unit. You have to carefully evaluate if making two pairs or three of a kind will help someone else make a bigger hand. This is an important part of advanced play in Hold 'Em.

Another circumstance in which to call with second pair is when you have other possibilities. For instance, you played this hand in late position with no raises:

and the flop comes:

Second pair with an inside straight draw and a back-door flush draw can be worth one call after the flop depending upon position and the amount of money in the pot. The best card to catch would be another eight. Catching a nine gives you a straight but it could give someone a better straight if they played a Queen-ten. There is some profit potential in this situation, but care must be taken.

Here is another illustration in which you might continue to play. This is your hand in late position:

This is not a hand to call a raise with, but I will certainly play it in an unraised pot. Sometimes that eight is a big enough kicker if an Ace comes, but it is not usually a big profit hand unless you hit the clubs. Anyway suppose you play and you catch this flop:

If there is a decent amount of money in the pot and only one betting unit to call, it might be okay to peal a card. Second pair with an overcard and a backdoor nut flush draw combine to make a marginal situation. The best card would be another eight, preferably the eight of hearts.

This flop is also a possible call:

You do not want to pair your eight now, but either a nine or an Ace would be good cards. However, beware a straight already made.

This flop would not be a good call for the A♣-8♣:

That heart flush draw makes a call here too risky. Some very good Hold 'Em players will not draw for a straight when the board has two cards of one suit.

FIGURE THE DRAWS

Figuring what draws are likely out against you and who has them is where we get into the more advanced form of play. The betting strategies for flopping the top pair and the monster hands are pretty easy. Figuring the draws and knowing the players is where the advanced player makes his money. There are some flops you can bet the hell out of and others to stay far away from. Knowing which is which is where the skill lies.

On every flop you are involved with you should have a good idea as to which possible draws are against you. This is especially true if you have the top pair, two pairs or trips. It is the draws that could beat you. Know what to look for if a trouble card comes, you can make a better decision. There are the obvious things to note on the flop, like flush draws. Others have obvious straight draws. Those are uncomplicated.

If you should play a hand like:

and the flop comes:

you don't have a problem with draws. Either you make the nut club draw or you don't. If a straight gets there and you make your flush, rejoice because you will have at least one caller.

When you see the flop, try to figure who has what draw or draws after the betting round and you see who is staying in. Try to figure the most likely draw, the long shot draw(s) like the inside straight draw and backdoor flush draw, and then the draw where a person has caught a part of the flop like second or third pair and has a draw to something else. All of these are hard to read when there are many callers, as so often happens in low-limit. Anyone can figure the flush draws, but it is the straight draws that demand the most study. Straight draws are no problem when there are three or four parts of it on the board. However, a flop like this is more difficult:

It is very common for at least two players to be drawing at inside straights. Say one had a nine-seven and another a six-nine. Of course, there is the possible open-ended straight draw with the six-seven. If you had big slick and therefore had top pair, there are a lot of cards that would be dangerous. Any eight, seven, six, four, nine or ten could make a straight for someone. I certainly don't have to remind you again of how important position is when you catch a perilous flop.

One of the main sources of income at the poker table should be when you recognize that the opponents are drawing at straights and flushes and don't make them. A bet on the end, even if you have very little or nothing, will often pull down the pot. If you are in late position and the other players have been checking and calling, indicating draw hands, and you have been betting, a bet on the end might be appropriate. If everyone missed their draws, one by one they will sigh and throw their hand away. When that happens, don't show them your busted flush draw. Just stack the chips. This is simply another example of advanced play and the power of position. Here is where you get paid off for being observant and knowing just a tad more about what the exciting game of Texas Hold 'Em is about. The main source of enrichment comes from the money we win, but it sure is fun to know that we play the game the way it should be played.

PLAYING THE NUT FLUSH DRAW

This is not an example of advanced play but I find this a fun time when I am drawing at the nut flush after the flop. One does not have to be a rocket scientist to max out the nut flush draws. There are only a few times when you cannot call and a lot of times when you can raise on the come and disguise your hand. This is a real fun time and you either make it or you don't.

41

Say you play:

and catch a flop like:

Depending upon your position you can call all raises if there are at least two other people in the pot. If there are four or five other players, you can often get in a raise. You have the nut flush draw and one overcard that could also win for you if it should come. This might be a place to check-raise if you are in early position to increase the size of the pot. I will often put in a raise on fourth street if my flush card does not come. This will really confuse the opponents. If one of my flush cards comes on the river, I can either get in a check-raise or get one or more callers than I could expect.

The danger in the above flop is that the board would pair with the four of clubs, giving someone a full house. Otherwise you either have the winning hand or you can throw the busted flush away. (Unless you have caught an Ace and think it might be the best hand.)

When shouldn't you call when you have the nut flush draw? Say we have the same hand:

and the flop comes:

Now that is a precarious flop. You can easily be up against a full house already and be drawing dead. However, you can call unless the betting is real heavy. The danger becomes suicide if on fourth street this card comes:

You are now done with the hand. Your great hand has turned to junk. Save your money and dump the hand.

In summary, there are three prime considerations for calling and betting when you catch a big piece or little piece of the flop:

1. The size of the pot

2. Your position

3. The abilities of your opponents and how you read them.

CHAPTER THREE

PLAYING THE PLAYERS

Now we get to the meat of it. Many things are important to a profitable career as a poker player: emotional control, patience, money management, knowledge of starting hands and the correct playing of position. You must combine them all into a mix that will win for you. However, there is one ingredient that flavors the mix, the salt, if you will, that brings it all together. That component is the knowledge of the human being(s) active in the pot. You must have command of what the other players are doing or reacting to at that particular moment, under those particular circumstances. What makes this so challenging is that there is no way to predict in advance what will happen. It is like the impossibility of stepping into the same river twice. From instant to instant the river changes. So do the players in a poker game. There is no possible

45

way for the same event to happen twice. Even if the cards should be dealt in exactly the same way, the players change from hand to hand. Someone has won the pot, others have lost. Their moods and outlooks change with each and every event. Consequently their reactions might change. As I mentioned, this is the meat of winning poker. Playing the players is the salt, the component that draws all the other ingredients together.

What can we do to try to grasp the major share of what is happening to our opponents? If the game is ten-handed, trying to keep current with nine opponents is a daunting task. However, there are some things we can do. Let me tell you what I generally do and perhaps you can clue off of that for your own techniques.

The first thing I try to do is put each player into a big category. The less I know about a player, the bigger the category. As I get to know him or her better, that category gets smaller and smaller. Let me see if I can explain this.

BAD OR GOOD

"Bad or good" is my first category. Suppose I sit down in a game of Hold 'Em with nine complete strangers. How do I go about placing the players into categories I can deal with?

The first question in my mind is who is a good player and who isn't. Who understands the game and who is just learning or stumbling around?

One clue is just the way a person handles the chips. Do they appear to be familiar with the chips? Do they pick them up and handle them with ease? Do they make easy moves with the chips as they bet? However, even if a person can take a stack of chips in one hand, separate them into two groups and riffle them back into one stack again does not make that person a good player. But it does tell me that the player is experienced at the table. Maybe he can't play worth a darn, but I will give him or her credit at that point for being experienced. Remember, I am only trying to separate each player into the good-player or bad-player section. So the first thing I do at a table with strangers is glance around the table and watch those players who are handling chips. Even before the cards are dealt, I have started to get a grasp on the different players.

The next thing I notice is how each player holds his cards. Do they peek at them and never look at them again? That tells me the player has the potential to be a good player. If a player has to go back and look at his cards again and again, he likely is a novice. The good player memorizes his cards and does not have to look again. I also notice how familiar the player is with the cards. Do they peek under at the correct corner to see what they have? Do they shield the cards effectively so that no one else can see? Is this peeking done in a effortless manner?

By this time I have made some preliminary judgments about the skill level of several players. From here on I will watch how well they play the hands. The first two clues, handling of chips and cards, are just preparatory.

A good player will simply not play very many hands. I sort of pride myself in being able to spot the good and bad players within one round of play. This isn't always true, but I feel I can come pretty close. For instance, if a person throws away six or seven hands out of ten, I will give him credit for being a good player. If he or she watches the action with intensity, I also place them in the good category.

If I notice a player who plays six or seven hands out of ten, I start by placing them in the bad category, waiting further review. I also notice the action of the hands when a player is waiting his turn to act. If they pick up the chips necessary to call before it is their turn to act, I place them in the bad category. When a player does that, he is giving a clue to others at the table.

Here is a very big clue. If I see a player pick up the number of chips necessary to *call* and then a player in front of them raises, and they go back to their stack to get more chips, this tells me that the player is a bad player. If they had cards strong enough to call a raise, they should have been raising with those cards. That action on their part tells me they do not understand the game of Hold 'Em. The number one sin of novice players is their hand selection.

Obviously, the best information you can get about each player is when they turn a hand over and you can re-create that hand in your mind. Did they play their cards well or were they just lucky? Was it appropriate for them to call a raise from that position, given that flop? Did they have a good draw? Did they maybe draw for a draw? Is the player cognizant of which players are good players or does he simply not care? These, and many other questions, should be asked.

FURTHER DEFINITIONS

Almost immediately I make finer definitions of the players. I have noticed that my good player category is pretty simple, there are only two sub-categories. There is only the good player and the very good player. It usually takes me an hour or so to put someone into the very good player group, but it can happen on the first hand. It depends whether that particular player shows down a hand that was superbly played. I will instantly tuck that player into the super category subject to review on his next revealed hand.

The bad classification has the sub-categories of:
* Novice
* Novice trying to learn
* Hopeless
* Hopeless with big bankroll
* Terrible
* Insane or "I give to charity"
* "I play to have fun, to hell with the money."

The last two categories are almost the same. However, I have found the last grouping the most fun to play with. You could be playing with a tourist only in town for a short time who has a bankroll he wants to distribute.

Whatever grouping you place the player, you will just love to have them at your table. Even if a player gets hot and wins some of your chips, you have an excellent chance to take back your money and a good bit of their money.

OTHER IMPORTANT CATEGORIES

After you have assigned each player to a group, now comes the tedious task of refining individual quirks and idiosyncracies. This is where you can begin to make moves that will either make you money or keep you from losing money. For instance, identify the players who will play an Ace with any sidecard, such as Ace-three offsuit in any position. Now suppose you are in the back and raise with:

and the flop comes:

Everyone checks to you, so you bet and get two callers, one of the caller is the guy who will play any Ace. Unless you improve on the next card, do not bet on the turn. The guy who plays that rag hand of Ace with bad kicker will surely call you down. If you do not improve on the river and he bets, dump the hand. He plays trash and once in a while will beat you with it. The information of who will play Ace-anything is an important clue.

What you are waiting for is to catch the Ace-big card and raise and catch an Ace on the flop. Now the guy is trapped into calling you down and his only shot is if he should hit his kicker and you do not. Sometimes the guys who play Ace-anything will even raise you when they catch an Ace on the flop. If you have a solid hand of Ace-big card, call them down unless the flop turns really nasty like four cards to a straight or flush and you don't have the right cards.

PLAYERS WHO MISPLAY THE BIG PAIRS

It is rare in low-limit poker that I will not raise when I catch one of the top three pairs. I will always raise with them in early and early middle positions. I simply cannot let players limp in behind me who might catch a big flop and cost me a lot of money. If they are going to play rags, they will have to pay. You will, however, find quite a number of players who will simply call with the big pairs. Most of these players will re-raise if the pot gets raised after they have acted. This tactic seldom will drive people out of the pot because they already have one or two betting units already invested. The conventional wisdom on playing the big pairs is to try to eliminate as many opponents as possible. They play best against one or two opponents.

My advice when you encounter someone who will slow-play a big pair is to retire from the action if you must pay two or more betting units to call. If you are the person who raised and got the back-raise, call the raise and hope to catch a big hand on the flop. You are probably going uphill, but you might get lucky.

Be especially cautious of getting into a raising war with less than a premium hand. Sometimes, after a back-raise, another player will put in the third raise, and if more than three raises are permitted, the pot will get capped off. These pots get huge and if you have some high suited cards, this could be a great opportunity to pull in a big pot.

Keep in mind that the player with the big pair is letting you get in cheap with a average-to-marginal hand for a cheap price. He is giving you a big break. It is only when that pot gets raised behind you and he re-raises that you are at a disadvantage. When the pot is not raised you will be given an almost free shot to take down their big pairs.

There is another group of players who will make a back-raise with any two suited cards or a low pair. They are gambling and you should be able to spot their play from earlier action. They are not usually like the guys who slow-play a big pair. The big-hand slow players are more conservative and tend to be calling stations. The guys with the tendency to back-raise with any two suited cards or small pairs are fun to have in the game. They are not conservative at all because they love to gamble. Once in a while they will pull in a pot, but in general will contribute substantially to your bank account.

My recommendation on the way to handle these guys is to put in another raise if you have good cards. Make them pay to do this kind of foolishness. They hate to be challenged like this and if you come right back at them it could very well set them on tilt.

WATCH FOR CHANGES

As I wrote about in the chapter on emotional control, there are many things that affect the average poker player. A long run of poor cards will often discourage a player. Watch for that and notice how his or her confidence goes down. They will look at their diminishing stack of chips and try to protect against any further losses. This might be a good time to check-raise and set them on tilt.

Beware of someone running very well. Try to avoid direct conflict unless you have an above average hand.

Mood swings are clearly a part of this game so watch each player and see how they are affected and how you can take advantage of these swings.

PREDICTING HANDS

An excellent exercise for all players is to make predictions as to what cards an opponent is holding. Predicting hands of good players is quite easy after a bit. The real challenge is becoming accurate with average and poor players. If you can get even 30 or 40% correct, you are doing well. There are some clowns who will become overly aggressive with a marginal hand when challenged by a raiser. They will just call the blind bet with any two suited cards but if someone has the audacity to raise in late position they will respond with a back-raise. Some players will also do this with the small pairs, hoping to catch the trip card on the flop. However, they usually get trapped into staying until the end in the hope of catching their magic card. They can burn you, but in the long run they are losers with this strategy.

CONSTANT UPDATING

I like to do a re-evaluation after each hand is played to update my predictions. Because of the ebb and flow of the game, my prediction game has to be updated. Some players hardly ever change, others swing like branches in a heavy wind. I feel I need to keep track of these changes as I look for ways to exploit them.

CHAPTER FOUR

TOOLS OF THE TRADE

A boxer has certain weapons that he carries into the ring. Some of his weapons are better than others. If he is a good boxer, he uses all of his weapons or tools to defeat the opponent. His left hook might be what he depends on to put away an opponent while his right jab is used to set up the hook or the uppercut. He also knows that training and footwork are critical to the final outcome. As he is training, he is well aware that he must fine tune his tools. He also knows that a positive mental attitude is critical tool for winning. The accomplished boxer knows how to use these tools to win.

The same thing is true for almost any sport. It takes a lot of work to become the good player. The better players know how to use the tools of their trade because they work hard polishing their skills. It goes beyond sports to business. The deal maker has tools that are vital for success. He or she must have a powerful sense of timing, a reliable knowledge of human nature and a sense of where opponents hot buttons are.

The advanced poker player, by definition, must have a good command of his tools. Let's take a quick look at some of these tools.

STABILITY

The advanced player is the person who is well on his way to mastering his craft. First, above all things, is his emotional control. Seldom does he or she get upset or go on tilt. He truly accepts the idiosyncrasies of low-limit poker. When another player makes an incredibly stupid move, (such as calling a couple of raises with a K-2 offsuit and winning the pot against our hero, who just happens to have pocket Queens and flops a set), the advanced player just eases back in his chair and waits for his turn. He knows the chips that bad player has just won are not locked up and he has a very good chance of recovering his loss, plus a good deal more.

PATIENCE

I have written extensively about patience in other books and articles. Without patience, one cannot become an advanced poker player. There it is. Straight out, no frills. A strong measure of patience is an absolute. Without patience, the poker player will be a loser.

Patience is a relative term. How much patience is enough? How can we measure patience? When can we say to ourselves, "I have patience at the poker table?" Those are tough questions.

My answer is that an advance player must be able to sit quietly for hours, yes, hours, waiting for the right starting hand in the right position in the correct circumstances. He not only must sit quietly, he must not complain like most players do. He knows the cards will come and so he waits. He does not piddle away his chips trying to make marginal hands work from a marginal position. The advanced player does not gripe about the dealer's inability to deliver him a playable hand. He simply waits for the drought to pass.

Patience, my friend, is a condition of profit and a rite of passage into the advanced class.

PROPER STARTING HAND SELECTION

Good hand selection is something that is learned at the basic and intermediate level. Good hand selection is tied together with patience and the power of position; the patience to wait for the good cards and knowing which cards can be played in all the positions.

AGGRESSIVE BETTING

A hallmark of an advanced player is his betting patterns. He is brutal when he gets the right cards. This is a very useful and profitable tool. When he finally gets the exact combination of cards in his hand and cards on the flop, he can make your hair bleed. He will bet, raise, or re-raise to get the maximum amount of money in the pot. It is scary to watch a master at work.

I am reminded of a jungle cat. The cat waits and watches for hours if necessary. When the prey is finally in the position for a kill, the cat's every sense is alert, every nerve ready to strike.

The advanced player waits until just the right time to spring into action. He will not change expression or give any outward indication that he is ready to spring. Suddenly, his calculations made, he acts with intensity and power. He throws the challenge at the feet of his opponents. The message is, "Call this, if you don't like money."

The advanced player also knows that there are times when it is smart to refrain from being aggressive. If one or more other players are taking the lead in betting and/or raising, the advanced player will often wait. He is aware that the other players respect his play and if he raises in the early going, he will scare off some prospective callers. Therefore he waits until near the end of the betting process to enter the fray.

Referring to the last chapter, Playing The Players, when you observe another advanced player putting in a raise at the end, beware. He likely has the nuts, and he has just played the hand to perfection and will reap the rewards of advanced play.

The advanced player has a sense of what is appropriate. He has learned when and how to make an aggressive move and when and how he will make the most money by laying back. When he has the winner, it becomes his custom to maximize the amount of money in the pot. He has put each and every player on the correct hand. He is never foolish by investing his chips where he does not have the best draw or the best hand. When he bets, raises or calls, expect him to pull in the pot.

FLEXIBILITY AT THE TABLE

One of the challenges of playing winning poker is being able to adapt to different types of games. I am not referring here to different games like stud or draw, but to the way a game of Hold 'Em can change from hour to hour or the differences in local situations. For instance, the usual low-limit poker game in Las Vegas is played somewhat differently in California club rooms. The players approach the game differently, the rake and blind structures are different, the house rules are not quite the same. I have also found that the play is often differs from card room to card room in the same town. For instance, some card rooms have a low opening bet, allowing the good player to play some marginal hands he normally would discard. The advanced player knows he is better at reading the flop than the other players, so he takes advantage of this opportunity to see more flops than usual.

It is also quite common for a game to change texture during the course of a session. As old players leave and new players come into the game, the tenor can change. The game can get tighter, looser, faster. Some of these changes must be noted and modifications made to maximize your possibilites for profit.

The game can suddenly become shorthanded. From ten players who love to play, four of the loosest players leave. Now you have five opponents, three who are pretty tight players. What to do? Should you pick up your chips and leave also? That might be a good alternative if you are tired or can find another game that offers good profit potential. However, if you are fresh and think you are better than the other players, you can adjust your play and take home some chips. The average winning hand decreases with the number of players and the power of intimidation becomes greater against conservative players. The advanced player should be able to adjust to all the possibilities. This ability is just one of the tools he needs in order to be successful.

FINDING NEW EDGES

Becoming the best player wherever you play is a matter of finding and implementing the small advantages. Having better emotional control is a huge edge. Having the most patience is another enormous edge. Good, solid hand selection is yet another major edge. These are just some examples of the bigger advantages. These edges should be started in the beginning and intermediate stages of poker skill.

The advanced player is looking for the smaller edges. With careful observation, you can develop some strategies that will give you just a few percentage points advantage over your opponents. "Why bother," you ask, "if there is only a small edge in these strategies." Here is why. Poker, being a game of skill, allows the skillful player to develop these small edges. Maybe it's only one or two percent. Maybe three or four. That isn't much, but as you grow and learn how to observe the game, you will discover more edges and add to your percentages. Soon you will have a 10% edge on your opponents. Over the course of a year, that could wind up being big money.

There is still another benefit from finding the edges. The beauty of doing so is that you will discover a whole new way of observing the game and the players. A little bit here, a big chuck there, and you will astonish yourself as to how much you will be able to scrutinize and add to your advantages. Each discovery opens the door to more discoveries.

I wish I could tell you how much each strategy or observation is worth in terms of percentages over your opponents. I can't do that because I don't know the sophistication of your opponents. They might have little knowledge of the game or they could be very, very good.

CONFIDENCE

I like the way my Webster's Collegiate defines *confidence*:

A state of mind or a manner marked by easy coolness and freedom from uncertainty.

Contrast that description with how Webster defines *arrogance*:

A feeling or an impression of superiority manifested in an overbearing manner or presumptuous claims.

We have all seen a flamboyant fellow sit down with a rack or more of chips and try to dominate the game. I find his manner obnoxious. This is far different than the person who quietly sizes up his opponents and with an "easy coolness" destroys the game because he really knows what he is doing. That man causes fear. His confidence in himself and his knowledge of the game are frightening. That is what I wish for you.

BETTING COURAGE

The advanced player is not timid. Even after several tough beats and a series of draws that do not materialize, he or she continues to wager chips on good hands. If the pot is raised a number of times and he holds a good hand, he does not flinch. His knowledge of the odds and the people involved verify his belief that his hand has the best chance to pull in the pot.

POWER OF OBSERVATION

This is a skill the advanced player has worked hard to develop. And he trusts his observations. Many players will see an action or reaction that they believe indicates a strong hand but don't have the conviction to throw their losing hand away. They just haven't learned to trust their power of observation yet.

These are only some of the tools of the trade for the good poker player. As with any good craft, the apprenticeship is quite long for the poker player. What is important is to just keep working on the tools until you *know* you are very good at this profession.

CHAPTER FIVE

CREATIVE FIXING

It is my belief that all top-notch poker players must have a powerful system whereby they can adjust their playing strategies and identify and correct their own playing errors. We all have heard players moan and carry on about how bad the cards are running. Some players will also criticize the stupidity of the other players. They will harangue the management of the card room staff and question the rules. They will complain about the food, the service and the heat. Count on it, my friend, none of those players are advanced Hold 'Em players! Advanced poker players do not have the time or the inclination to complain. They adjust. Plain and simple, they adjust. They accept the conditions, the staff, the cards and the other players. Sure, they recognize that life could be better if everything were perfect, but they don't expect a perfect world. So they adjust. They simply set about their task of winning money by accepting the world as it is and adjusting to that world. Their goal is winning and nothing will get in their way. In other words, they have developed a system of creatively fixing, or accommodating to their surroundings.

FIXING LEAKS IN YOUR GAME

This fixing must go on at several levels. All poker players develop leaks (playing habits that are not profitable) in their game. Lately I have fallen into the trap of playing the King-ten from early middle position. Sometimes I have won with that hand and that winning is intoxicating. Sometimes the number of players coming in without a raise makes it okay to play that King-ten, but it is still a bad habit, a leak in my game. Oh, I can justify it to myself. I can play all kinds of mental games, but the fact is that King-ten is a poor hand to play in any but the late positions.

How does one go about fixing a leak? The first step, naturally, is to identify a call or a play as a leak. Finding a starting hand like King-ten is fairly easy. Other leaks like drawing to the second pair from the wrong position, calling a raise with a hand with two picture cards that are not suited, calling with an inside straight draw when the pot does not justify it, or trying to "get" another player because he or she made you angry can occur as we get deeper into the game. It is easy to develop a leak or two, so we must do a careful analysis of our game and call a leak a leak. That is the first step.

Next, we must be constantly on the lookout and spot the leak as it is happening. When we can do that, it is simply a matter of will to re-evaluate the situation and probably discard the hand. Hundreds of times I have told students that the secret of winning at poker is in the wrist. *Cock that wrist and throw those losers away.*

A leak that a lot of players have, especially in low-limit poker, is playing too many hands. As one plays more Hold 'Em, the number of hands played will increase because you become more proficient in recognizing profitable situations after the flop. However, the playing of those hands must be done from late-middle and late position. Playing too many hands is intoxicating and can easily become a bad habit, or in other words, a leak. We must therefore be creative in our finding and eliminating our leaks.